THE Power OF PLANTS

Claire Llewellyn

OXFORD

UNIVERSITY PRESS

OXFORD
UNIVERSITY PRESS

Great Clarendon Street, Oxford OX2 6DP

Oxford University Press is a department of the University of Oxford.
It furthers the University's objective of excellence in research, scholarship,
and education by publishing worldwide in

Oxford   New York

Auckland   Cape Town   Dar es Salaam   Hong Kong   Karachi
Kuala Lumpur   Madrid   Melbourne   Mexico City   Nairobi
New Delhi   Shanghai   Taipei   Toronto

With offices in

Argentina   Austria   Brazil   Chile   Czech Republic   France   Greece
Guatemala   Hungary   Italy   Japan   Poland   Portugal   Singapore
South Korea   Switzerland   Thailand   Turkey   Ukraine   Vietnam

Oxford is a registered trade mark of Oxford University Press
in the UK and in certain other countries

British Library Cataloguing in Publication Data

Data available

ISBN 978-0-19-919847-4

20

Printed in China by Imago

Paper used in the production of this book is a natural,
recyclable product made from wood grown in sustainable forests.
The manufacturing process conforms to the environmental
regulations of the country of origin.

Acknowledgements

The publisher would like to thank the following for permission to reproduce
photographs: p4/5 MM Studios; p6 Corbis; p7 OUP; p8 MM Studios; p9 Picture Tasmania Photo
Library/photographers direct.com; p10 Brand X Pictures (top), Corbis/Richard Hamilton Smith
(bottom); p12 Corbis/Scott T Smith (top), Corbis/Farrell Grehan (bottom); p14 Getty/Altrendo
(top), Alamy (bottom left), Science Photo Library/ TH Foto-Werlung (bottom right); p15
MM Studios (all); p16 Science Photo Library/Dan Suzio (both); p17 Tzaud photo/photographers
direct.com; p18 Alamy/Photolibrary Wales (top), Getty/Photodisc Green (bottom); p19 Hotham
Primary School (all); p20 Corbis/Caron Philippe (top), Alamy/Garden Picture Library (bottom
left), Gillian Gunner/photographers direct.com (bottom right); p21 MM Studios (all); p22 Alamy/
Photobliss (left), Alamy/David Wootton (right); p23 Alamy/Jack Sullivan

Cover photo: Alamy

Additional photography by Oxford University Press

Illustrations by Martin Aston and Oxford Designers and Illustrators

The publisher would like to thank Gwyn Jones, Maggie Gunning and the children and staff
of Hotham Primary School for the photos on page 19.

Contents

Introduction 4

What are plants? 6

Plants feed us 8

Plants clothe us 10

Plants house us 12

Plants that can cure 14

Plants that can kill 16

Plants in the environment 18

A global garden 20

Record-breaking plants 22

Index & Glossary 24

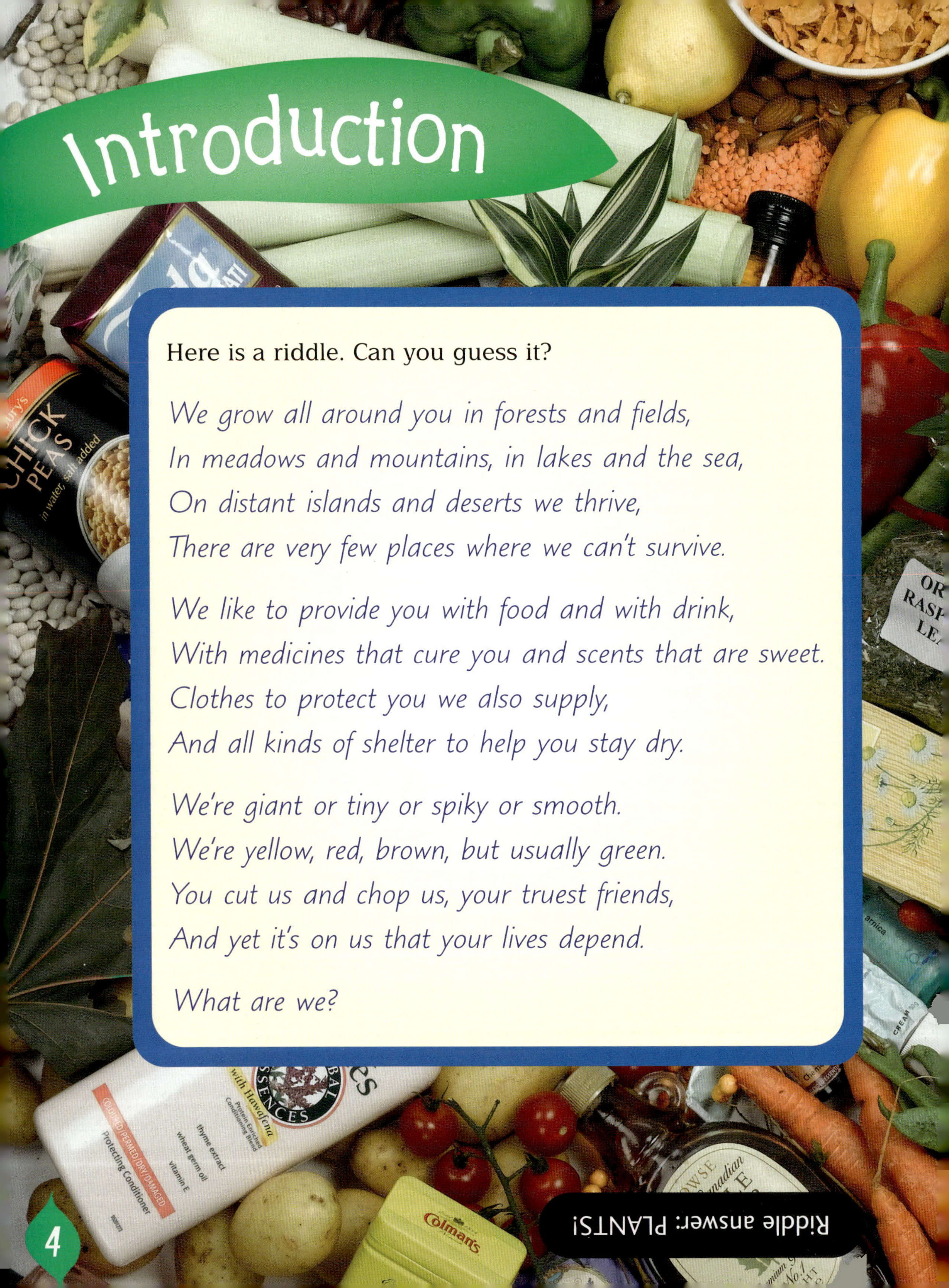

Here is a riddle. Can you guess it?

We grow all around you in forests and fields,
In meadows and mountains, in lakes and the sea,
On distant islands and deserts we thrive,
There are very few places where we can't survive.

We like to provide you with food and with drink,
With medicines that cure you and scents that are sweet.
Clothes to protect you we also supply,
And all kinds of shelter to help you stay dry.

We're giant or tiny or spiky or smooth.
We're yellow, red, brown, but usually green.
You cut us and chop us, your truest friends,
And yet it's on us that your lives depend.

What are we?

Riddle answer: PLANTS!

This book looks at many kinds of plants – some that you may know, and some you may not. It explains how plants grow, and celebrates the many different ways plants improve our lives.

What are plants?

Plants are living things. They cannot move around like animals but they are still very much alive. They grow, feed, make new plants and eventually die. A big difference between plants and animals is that plants do not have to search for food to eat: they can make it all by themselves.

Leaves make food for the plant. Without leaves, a plant cannot grow.

Stem sucks up water and carries it to other parts of the plant.

Roots take in water and goodness from the soil.

How plants grow

A plant needs light, water and warmth to grow. The roots, stem and leaves of the plant work together to help it survive.

Plants in action: See how plants grow

Method

- Fill the glass with soil.
- Plant the bean under the soil, near the side of the glass.
- Water the soil lightly and keep it damp.

Day 21

Day 1

Day 7

Plants feed us

People have always eaten plants. First, they picked wild plants. Then, thousands of years ago, people began to collect seeds from plants, and to sow them in the ground. This was the beginning of farming.

Plants provide us with many different foods

Fresh vegetables are tasty and full of goodness.

Herbs and spices flavour our food.

Cereals feed millions of people around the world.

Nuts are crunchy and good for you.

Fruits are sweet and juicy.

Mmm! Our favourite treats are made from plants.

Home or away?

Some foods are grown by local farmers in a particular season of the year. Others are grown in warmer places and brought to us on boats and planes. It's a good idea to buy local foods if you can. Can you think why? One reason is that it helps to reduce environmental pollution and possible damage to the climate if we cut down on the shipping or **air-freighting** of food.

QUICK QUIZ

Question: I was once a kind of wild grass but today I am grown on farms. My seeds are ground to make flour for pasta and bread. What am I?

Which of these foods are not grown where you live?

Grown locally: carrots, strawberries, sweetcorn, leeks

Grown overseas: rice, kiwi, pineapple, bananas

Quick Quiz Answer: Wheat

Plants clothe us

If you take a plant and pull it to pieces, you will see that it is made of stringy fibres. In some plants the fibres are soft and strong. They can be used to make cloth.

Making cotton

Many of our clothes are made from cotton. It is a very important cloth. The cotton plant grows in warm, dry places. Its fruits, called bolls, contain fluffy seeds. Their fibres can be spun into thread and woven into cloth. This is then dyed with different colours.

Colourful cotton

Farm machines harvesting cotton in a field in Mississippi, USA

Plants in action:

Make a vegetable dye

Almost any plant can produce a dye.
Why not use vegetables to dye a T-shirt?
Ask an adult to help you.

Materials

Choose from: beetroot
(red/purple), onion
skins (yellow/tan),
spinach (green)

Old white cotton
T-shirt

Equipment

- bowl
- chopping board
- knife
- large saucepan
- rubber gloves
- colander

Method

- Wash and cut up your vegetables.
- Put them in a bowl and add water to cover. Leave to stand overnight.
- Transfer the vegetables and water to a pot and simmer for 1 hour.
- Remove the vegetables, put in the T-shirt and simmer for 30 minutes.
- Turn off the heat, and leave to soak for 4 hours.
- Take out the T-shirt, rinse and dry.

Plants house us

Trees are made of a hard, woody material that is good for building. Wood holds up the roof and ceilings of a house, and often frames the windows and doors. Wood is smooth, warm and beautiful. It makes good-looking furniture and floors.

A simple wooden house

Building with bamboo

Bamboo is a tall grass with sturdy stems, which grows in warm, wet places. It is a very good material for building, and is cheap and easy to get hold of. It can be used for scaffolding.

Every part of this house is made of bamboo.

The walls are made of thin stems woven together.

Thicker stems hold up the house.

QUICK QUIZ

Question: I am a tree that can live for 1,000 years. My wood is strong and slow to rot. It has been used to build ships, churches, houses and furniture. What am I?

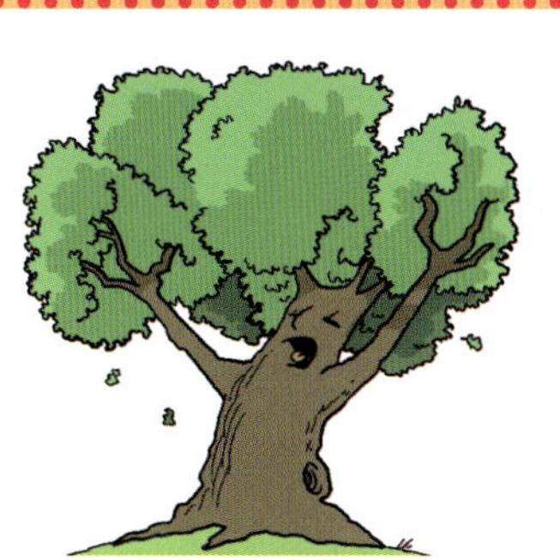

Many things in our homes are made from plants.

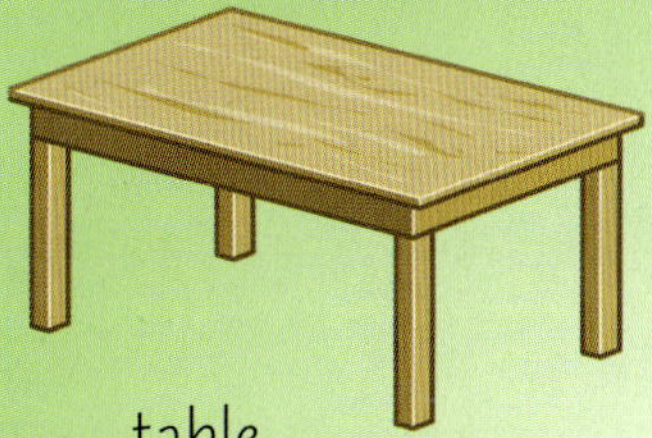

table

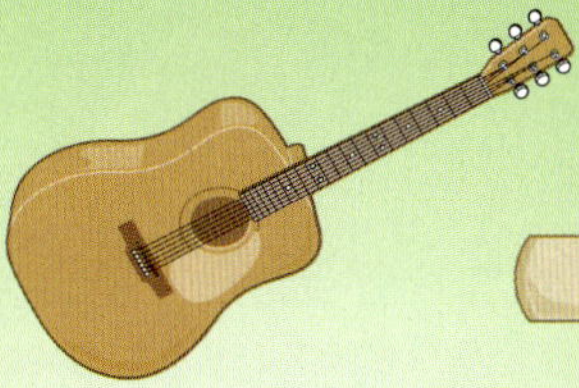

guitar

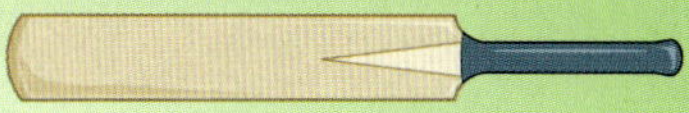

cricket bat

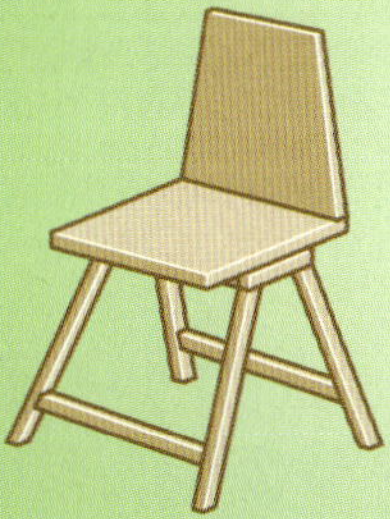

chair

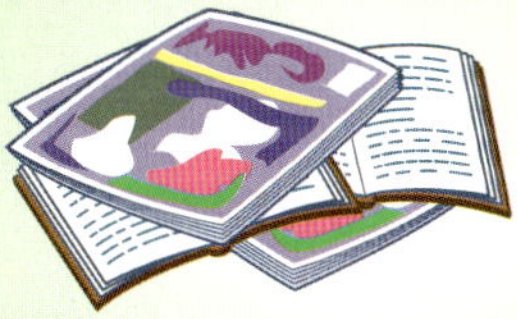

books, newspapers/magazines (made from wood pulp)

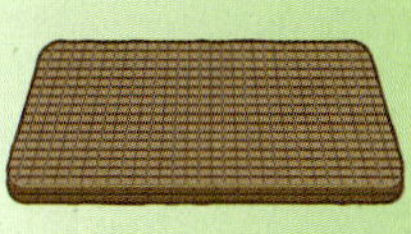

doormat (made from **coir**)

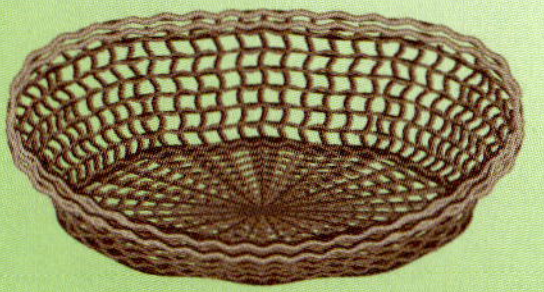

dog basket

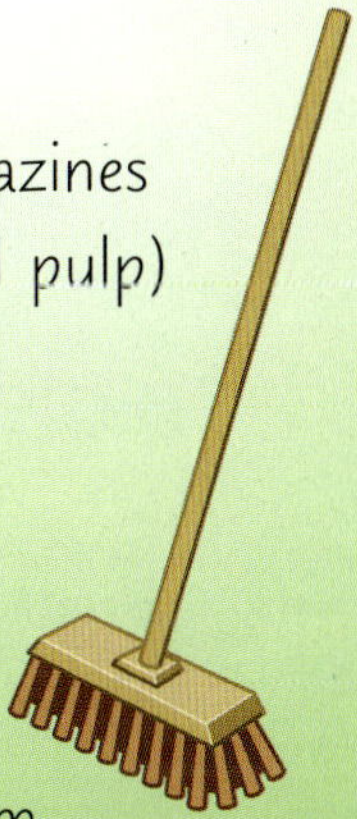

broom

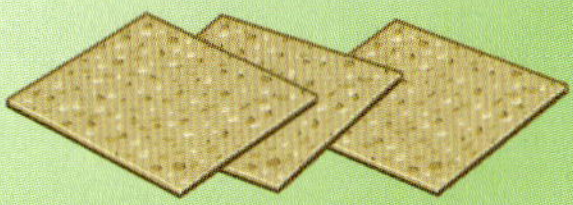

floor tiles (made from cork)

Quick Quiz Answer: An oak tree

Plants that can cure

Have you ever been stung by stinging nettles and rubbed a dock leaf on the sting? Some people think that the oils in the leaf help to soothe the pain. Many plants and herbs have the power to help us. They have been used for thousands of years to help cure illness, and scientists still use plants today.

Plant-astic!

Eucalyptus (say yoo-kal-ipp-tuss) oil is good for bad chests and blocked noses, and is used in cough medicines, too.

Clean and sweet

We also use plant oils to care for our bodies. Some oils clean away dirt and grease. Some are good for our hair and skin. Other oils have a wonderful scent and can be used in perfumes. All these oils make us feel great!

The oil of the sandalwood tree has a wonderful spicy smell!

Coconut oil softens the skin and makes hair shine.

Plants in action: Cure a tummy ache

Materials:
- mint plant
- water

Equipment:
- scissors
- kettle
- mug

Mint is a herb and is good for the stomach. Next time you or someone you know has a tummy ache, try making a cup of mint tea. Ask an adult to help you.

Method:

Cut a stem from the plant.

Wash the mint and put it in a mug.

Boil a kettle, then pour the water on the mint.

Leave to stand for 5–10 minutes, then slowly sip the tea.

QUICK QUIZ

Question: I grow in the garden. My purple-blue flowers have a sweet smell. They are used to make perfume and soap. What am I?

Plants that can kill

Plants are not always as harmless as they seem. The Venus fly-trap kills and eats flies. If a fly lands on one of its leaves, the two halves of the leaf snap shut. The trapped fly is bathed in a bitter juice. This changes its body to a gloopy soup, which the hungry plant soaks up.

Poisonous plants

Plants can also hurt larger animals. From time to time, cows, horses and even humans have died after eating poisonous plants. It is not just berries and mushrooms that can kill: roots, leaves, flowers and seeds can, too.

These plants are common and parts of them all are poisonous.

tulip/daffodil/hyacinth (bulbs)

foxglove (leaves)

buttercup
(all parts)

mistletoe (berries)

sweet pea
(seeds)

Warning

Never eat any part of a plant unless an adult tells you it is safe!

Many people grow rhubarb in their gardens. The pink, juicy stems are good to eat, but the leaves are poisonous.

Plant-astic!

Did you know that palm trees can be dangerous? If a ripe coconut fell on your head, it could kill you.

Plants in the environment

A lot of our world is covered in concrete. Our local environment – the streets and buildings – can look hard and grey. Plants are soft, green and alive. They can be used to brighten our surroundings, not only in our homes and gardens, but in our streets, schools and other public spaces. Wherever they are used, plants soften and improve our environment, and help wildlife.

A school playground

Many school playgrounds are covered in concrete. Some have no plants of any kind. How can they be improved? Hotham School had some big empty planters. By filling the planters with plants, the playground was improved. They also provided shelter and food for wildlife.

New plants were chosen to attract wildlife.

The children put new soil into the planters.

Everyone helped to look after the plants.

After one year, the planters were full of green plants.

Insects and other wildlife now visit the plants.

A global garden

Plants grow almost everywhere on Earth. They can grow where the climate is cold or hot. They can grow where it is wet or dry. Scientists tell us that there are at least 250,000 different plants on the planet – and many more are yet to be discovered!

The Eden Project

There is a place in Cornwall in England that celebrates plants. It is called the Eden Project. This global garden contains 5,000 plants from all over the world. Some have been planted outside and others in huge greenhouses, where the 'climates' can be controlled. One of the greenhouses is hot and steamy – just like a tropical rainforest.

This banana tree grows in the tropical greenhouse – along with 1,000 other kinds of plant.

Plants in action:

Grow greenhouse plants

A bottle garden is a mini-greenhouse. You can make one in a jar or bowl like this one.

Method:

Wash and dry the jar.

Put a layer of gravel (2 cm), a layer of charcoal (1 cm) and a layer of soil (8 cm) in the jar.

Plant your plants in the soil.

Water them lightly with a cup of water.

After a few days you should put plastic wrap over the jar.

Plant-astic!

The greenhouses at the Eden Project are the biggest in the world. One of them is 11 double-decker buses high, and could hold the Tower of London!

Record-breaking plants

Some plants stand out from all the others because they are the oldest, the tallest, the smallest or the smelliest! Read on to discover the record-breakers in the world of plants.

The world's biggest tree is a giant sequoia (say see-kwoy-a) in California, USA. This huge **conifer** is 84m tall – one-and-a-half times taller than Nelson's Column. And it's wide, too – a class of 30 children could hold hands around the 25-metre base.

The world's biggest flower grows in the rainforests of Asia. It is called the rafflesia (say raff-lee-sha), and measures nearly 1m wide. It is also said to be the smelliest flower: it stinks of rotting meat.

The bamboo plant is the fastest-growing plant in the world. One kind of bamboo can grow nearly 1m a day. It would reach the roof of a two-storey house in about a week.

The oldest plant alive today is a bristlecone pine tree in North America. The tree is more than 4,700 years old – as old as the pyramids in Egypt.

The slowest growing tree is a white cedar (say see-da) in Canada. Although it is 155 years old, it is only 10cm tall.

The coco-de-mer palm tree grows the world's biggest seeds. At 20kg they're as heavy as a large sack of potatoes.

The plant with the world's longest roots is the wild fig tree. Its roots grow 120m down into the soil. If the tree stood on a 40-storey building, its roots would reach down to the ground.

Index

bulb   17

cereal   8

charcoal   21

climate   20

concrete   18–19

conifer   22

dye   10–11

environment   18–19

fibre   10

global   20

herb   14

leaves   6, 16–17

local   7, 18

rainforest   20, 22

roots   6, 16

scent   14

seeds   10, 16–17

shoots   6–7

stem   6–7

woven   10

Glossary

air-freighting – transporting fresh food or other materials by plane

coir – the stiff outer fibres on a coconut shell

conifer – evergreen tree or shrub, such as a pine

cork – the tough outer tissue of the cork oak tree often used for bottle stoppers

espadrilles – a light canvas shoe with a sole made of plaited grass or rope